BURGE MEMORIAL TRUST

THE BURGE MEMORIAL TRUST was founded in 1926 to commemorate the work for International Friendship of the Right Rev. Hubert Murray Burge, formerly Bishop of Oxford and President of the World Alliance for promoting International Friendship through the Churches, and sometime Headmaster of Winchester College. The annual Burge Memorial Lecture is intended, in accordance with the terms of the Trust Deed, to forward the cause of international friendship through the Churches and to promote a better and wider understanding of the international obligations of Christian peoples. The first lecture was delivered in King's College, London, on May 10th, 1927, by Professor Sir Ernest Barker.

THE BURGE MEMORIAL LECTURE

CHRISTIANITY
AND THE
RECONCILIATION
OF THE
NATIONS

✳

C. H. DODD

Delivered in the
Great School, Westminster School
November 13th, 1951

SCM PRESS LTD
56 BLOOMSBURY STREET
LONDON

First published February 1952

Printed in Great Britain by
The Camelot Press Ltd., London and Southampton

CHRISTIANITY AND THE
RECONCILIATION OF THE NATIONS

✳

THE NEW TESTAMENT ends with a glowing picture of the destination of human history. There is a vast concourse before the throne of God, from every nation, tribe, people and language, and there is the Holy City, with all the nations bringing their glory and honour into it, and walking in the light of the city where night never falls.

Much labour, not all of it profitable, has been expended in attempts to decipher the mysterious imagery of the Book of Revelation. But from this passage at least we may safely deduce that Christianity recognizes the grouping of mankind according to nationality, race and language as a fact of history falling within the divine purpose, but not as an ultimate fact about man, since it is to be transcended as history reaches its goal. The clarity and decision with which the New Testament thus proclaims the unity of mankind before God, without denying or condemning the natural divisions which give character to its history, are specific marks of the Christian outlook.

Bearing this in mind, we have a clue to the value which the New Testament writers set upon the Church in its character as an international—or rather supra-national—society, in which there is 'neither Jew nor Greek, barbarian nor Scythian', but all are one in the body of Christ. That such a community should actually exist, in a world like this, is a theme to which they recur with wonder and delight. In this respect, as in others, the Church is treated as a kind of preliminary model, on a small and imperfect scale, of what the final state of mankind is to be in God's design. Thus a reference to the nations of the world, to their actual divisions and to their destined unity, is inherent in the very idea of the Church from the outset.

If we survey the centuries of Christian history, we must, I think, allow that the Church has never entirely lost sight of its supra-national vocation, though it has sometimes had a very uncertain grasp of it, and at other times has striven to assert it by means which have had the effect of increasing division. Sections of the Church, at disunion among themselves, have even become instruments of a divisive nationalism. It was so in the East when in the fifth century Syria went Nestorian and Egypt Monophysite, and prepared the way for the Mohammedan conquest. It was so in the sixteenth century when in the West national churches provided the framework for movements which tore Christendom into fragments. Yet the idea of a Christian world-community persisted, however ineffectually. Recently the tide has turned. We have seen an attempt made to restore ecumenicity to the separated churches of East and West alike; though Rome, with its own magnificent record as a supra-national society, elected to stand outside in an attitude of benevolent detachment. It was a stirring moment in the history of Christendom when representatives of Protestant and Orthodox churches from many lands assembled at Amsterdam to affirm their unity in Christ, and to devise machinery, through a World Council of Churches, for the expression and extension of that unity. Yet even at that moment there were ominous abstentions, and sombre warnings were uttered against the danger of papering over structural faults. They were only too well justified. Already the Christian communions in whole regions have renounced fellowship with the World Council—some of them perhaps cannot help themselves—and the term 'ecumenical' is subject to considerable discount. Once again we have learned that there is no short-cut.

Every such setback or disappointment means that

the Church has failed once again to be itself. The fault is not in our stars, but in ourselves; nothing human is exempt from the sin that wars in our members, and there is no discharge in that war. It is the part of faith to reaffirm, in the face of failure, the permanent character of the Church as the one people of God, and the 'earnest' of the ultimate reconciliation of all mankind. At a level deeper than all our divisions the unity already exists. Before the depressing spectacle of our divided world it is an alleviation to remember that on any given Sunday Christian people in every nation under heaven, separated on the earthly level by almost impassable barriers, have heard and said the same words of Gospel and Creed, and repeated the same sacramental acts. Those words and actions, unless they are mere meaningless form—and I doubt if they are ever *nothing* more than that—affirm our unity before God in spite of ourselves. In so far, the concourse before the throne of God out of every nation, tribe, people and language is a realized fact. That this thing does happen, in spite of the sins and errors of Christian people and Christian churches, is a continuing pledge that God's purpose for and through His Church is not foiled by our defections. Indeed at this very time there is evidence coming in, penetrating iron curtains and making itself heard above the mutual denunciations of ecclesiastical patriots, that the picture is even now not altogether misleading which a writer of the second century drew of the Church in the world:

'Christians are not to be distinguished from other men by country, language or customs. They have no cities of their own, they use no peculiar dialect, and they practise no extraordinary way of life. Residing in cities of the Greek world and beyond it, as is the lot of each, they follow the local customs in clothing, diet and general manner of life, but at the same time they exhibit the constitution of their own commonwealth as something quite paradoxical. They reside in their own homelands—but as aliens. Every foreign land is home to them, every homeland a place of exile. In a word, what the soul is in the body, Christians are in the world. The soul is dispersed through all the members of the body, and so are Christians among the cities of the world. The soul is enclosed in the body, but holds the body together, and Christians are enclosed in the world as in a prison, but it is they who hold the world in unity.'[1]

Perhaps we cannot at once adopt all this author's language for ourselves. The sense of being imprisoned in a hostile world, and the detachment of the

[1] *Epistle to Diognetus,* 5–6, abridged.

Christian from his native land, understandable enough in the second century, may seem to us overdone; yet there are contemporary situations in which both are strictly true to the experience of Christian people, and perhaps in the last resort they are inseparable from the mission of the Church in history. In essentials, it is this same conception of the Church that informs the ecumenical movement of our own time. That movement is in the first place an effort of Christian people to restore fellowship among themselves. We may now consider what bearing this idea of the unity of the Church may have upon the problem of uniting the nations of the world.

The main reason why it is significant that the Church maintains its unity in gospel and sacrament, which to the practical man may seem irrelevant to the realities of our situation, is that it bears permanent witness to the belief, which is quite fundamental, and should make itself felt in all Christian intervention in the world of affairs, that the work of reconciling mankind is God's work and not ours, to be accomplished on His terms, not ours, and in the end by His power and wisdom, and not by any such material strength or scientific knowledge and skill as we may achieve, though human power and wisdom may be used in furthering the divine purpose.

For while the Church is primarily a symbol of the

[10]

purpose of God to unite mankind, it is also designed to be an instrument of that purpose, and an instrument employed in strict accordance with the nature of the end in view. Its characteristic method of working may perhaps be brought out if we pursue the somewhat quaint illustration offered by the writer I have quoted. The Church in the world is like the soul in the body. I take it he is thinking of the 'soul' as a kind of organic principle governing the growth, nutrition, and functioning of all parts of the body in the interests of the life of the organism as a whole. The implication is that the Church represents and embodies a principle which transforms society from within; and further—for this too is implied in the metaphor—that its power to transform is dependent on its close identification with any particular part of the body of mankind in which it may reside. It is for this reason that our writer emphasizes the fact that Christians follow the local customs of the place where they live, and in doing so are in the way of performing their true function. We may extend what he says, and say that the Church is in the way of helping forward the reconciliation of nations in proportion as its members in any nation genuinely share in the national traditions, culture and institutions. For it is then in a position to make use of the natural network of human relations for its work of permeating society from within.

[11]

Upon this point there is a passage in the epistles of Paul which I think has not received sufficient attention. It is where he is discussing marriage and the family, in the seventh chapter of the First Epistle to the Corinthians. Here he has occasion to consider the burning question of mixed marriages, and he lays it down that a pagan husband married to a Christian wife (or *vice versa*) is made 'holy' by the union, and that the children of such marriages are themselves 'holy' simply because one of their parents is Christian. By the term 'holy' Paul does not, of course, mean 'extremely virtuous', as we often do. 'Holy' means for him, as for other writers of the New Testament, standing within that special relation to God set up by the work of Christ. It means belonging, in some sense, to the people of God. It is surely a striking fact that Paul could say that a man who himself remains a pagan becomes in some sense one of God's people simply through his marriage with a Christian woman, and that their children, from birth on, belong to God. There is such a thing as a Christian family, even though not all its members are Christians. Even so they bear, in some sort, the Christian stamp. The implication seems to be that the natural ties of marriage and parenthood are, in God's design, by reason of their power and intimacy, means by which the total effect of His work for mankind in Christ may be diffused through human society at large.

If so, I believe we should be justified in extending the principle from the family to the nation. For the ties which bind members of one nation are analogous to those which unite a family: partly physical (blood and soil), partly psychological (the effect of geography and inheritance on disposition and mentality) and partly ideal (patriotism and loyalty to the national tradition). If Paul can say that the unbelieving husband is 'made holy' by the believing wife, then it would seem legitimate to say that the non-Christian part of a country's population is 'made holy' in the same sense by intimate daily association with their Christian fellow-citizens or fellow-subjects. It is this fact that justifies the conception of a 'Christian nation'. It is not absurd to apply that term to some European nations, even though large numbers of their people do not hold the Christian faith, because the process of permeation has proceeded over a long period, and resulted in establishing at any rate certain minimal Christian assumptions as part of the national make-up. There is even evidence, set forth for example in Latourette's great book on *The Expansion of Christianity*, that the influence of a small Christian minority can affect the ethos of a whole people, without most of them being at all aware of it. What

I suspect has been and still is largely lacking in the impact of Christianity upon the Christian nation (especially perhaps in Protestant countries) is the distinct awareness that to be a Christian implies not only the attempt seriously to practise the Christian virtues in private life, and in family and civic relations, but also to think, feel and behave as a citizen of a world-community. Ecumenicity is inseparable from genuine Christianity. Perhaps few Christian people *really* believe that. To extend, deepen and strengthen the belief would be a powerful contribution to the cause of reconciliation among nations.

Can we go further in defining what the Christian community may do, individually and corporately, for that cause? I do not believe it is profitable to attempt to frame precise Christian directives, based immediately on the New Testament or upon pure Christian principle. It is the part of the Christian man to further, as he has opportunity, any movement or agency which an honest and intelligent person can believe to tend towards international peace and understanding. He will do so always with the consciousness that our human ability to know and to do what is right is limited, and he will take responsibility for the wrong that may be done in the effort to do right. He can afford to do so, because he believes that the divine forgiveness can deal with the wrong, that God's purpose may be served by the failure or by the success of our efforts, and that all those efforts are in the long run subject to the over-ruling purpose of God 'to sum up all things in Christ'. Christians therefore may be prepared for a proper kind of opportunism which rejects any rigidly doctrinaire approach to our problem.

If we were to look for any more precise guidance from the New Testament upon the concrete international situation in which we are at present involved, we should be likely to feel some disappointment. For its writers, though they constantly have 'the nations' in view, in the lump, show little disposition to consider individual nations in their concrete historical existence, as we have to consider them. There was good reason for this. The nation-state as we know it —and it is the nation-state that we normally have in mind when we speak of the reconciliation of nations as a political problem—was not within the purview of the primitive Christians. Indeed it can hardly be said to have existed in the ancient world, in any form like that which constitutes our problem at the present day. There were tribes and amalgamations of tribes, city-states and federations of city-states (usually very unstable), and beyond that there were empires, created and maintained through the power wielded by an individual ruler. Of all the empires of the ancient world, the Roman had best succeeded in turning empire into something like a commonwealth of nations. The nations did bring their glory and honour into Rome, and walk in her light—a light however whose evening was hastening on.

The early Church grew up within the empire. Even if its members had possessed the political authority and responsibility which was denied them, they had not to face the problem of reconciling nations with one another (with one exception which we shall notice presently). Rome had done that, in her rough-and-ready, often brutal, but fairly effective way. Thus in one aspect of the matter, the early Church contemplated the problem of the nations from a stage of political evolution a step beyond our present achievement. We are endeavouring, with indifferent success so far, to build a supra-national community organized under a single authority. Rome had done it. The *Pax Romana*, though disturbed from time to time, was a reality. Within the Roman world-state there was no race problem. Europeans, Asiatics and Africans could and did hold the highest offices on equal terms, and even ascend the imperial throne. Trade and industry were organized with no regard for national frontiers. A common culture was shared by men of every race. A common loyalty bound all together. The soldier of the empire might be a Briton, a German or an Arab, but on the remotest frontier he could reflect with pride, 'All the earth is Roman earth, and I shall die in Rome'.

Consequently, for the Christian of the first century the idea of a world-community was an easy one to entertain. It was an idea realized in the actual political structure within which he lived: 'the kingdom of the world', as it is called in the New Testament. For us the nation-state represents the norm of political organization. The supra-national world-state is still a utopian vision, hovering just beyond the limits of the practical. For the early Church, therefore, the problem was not, in the main, that of uniting nations, but of bringing the existing United Nations Organization under a new sovereignty: 'the kingdom of this world is become the kingdom of our God and of His Christ'.[1] The change contemplated was no doubt momentous. Yet it did not appear necessarily to involve any substantial change of *structure*. In reality the problem was less simple. The very efficiency of the Roman power suppressed or concealed, while it lasted, some of the most potent factors in the situation, which after its collapse would assert themselves, and in course of time create the intractable problem of the sovereign nation-state.

[1] Rev. 11.15.

It is, however, particularly instructive for us to observe that Christian critics of ancient society, while they often gave generous recognition to the services the empire rendered to justice and good order among men, felt compelled to renounce its claim to ultimate authority. For Augustine, writing as the empire in the West was tottering to its fall, Rome has come to stand for that *civitas terrena,* that earthly state, founded upon love of self amounting to contempt of God, which is eternally set over against the City of God, founded upon love of God amounting to contempt of self. His penetrating analysis of the moving impulses of the *civitas terrena,* exemplified from the Old Testament and from Roman history, stands as a permanent exposure of the inherent self-destructiveness of political organizations, however grandiose in their conception, which rest upon false foundations. The lesson for us is clear. The mere fact of uniting many nations in one organization and under one authority is not in itself that reconciliation of the nations which Christianity means. It is quite possible for 'the parliament of man, the federation of the world', supposing it to be attained, whether directed from the Kremlin or from Flushing Meadows, to serve the ends of Antichrist, and to serve them far more effectively than divided nations ever could. It is important that criticism by Christian principles should be directed upon all such schemes—not so much upon their machinery as upon the values underlying their formulation, and upon the relation of means to ends.

How are we to define such principles, in so far as they may be supposed applicable to international affairs? If we speak of justice, mercy and truth, it may be said that we are only re-stating the universal 'law of nature' common to all men. That law, according to the Epistle to the Romans, is 'written upon the heart' even of the heathen.[1] It is certainly part of the mission of the Church to bear witness to it, illuminated as it is by the further revelation in Christ—and it is especially its mission to do so at a time when some nations expressly repudiate it. Yet such principles are extremely general, and do not bring us very far on our way. If on the other hand the Church were to feel itself bound to urge upon nations the specifically Christian precepts of the Sermon on the Mount, it might find itself demanding of non-Christians a conformity to the highest ideal which it has never yet been able fully to secure from its own members. I do not here propose to enter upon the difficult problem I have adumbrated; for I believe that without raising such ultimate questions it is possible to recover from the New Testament itself some more direct light upon the quality required of any valid work of

[1] Rom. 2.15.

reconciliation, and the conditions it presupposes.

I said that the national state as we know it did not come within the purview of early Christianity, and that nations, in our sense of the term, can hardly be said to have existed at the time when the Church began its work in the world. Yet there was within the Roman Empire one people which showed at any rate many of the marks of a nation in the full sense. The Jews were a people priding themselves on community of blood, intensely attached to the soil of their country, with a long tradition of independence, devoted to a native culture, cherishing in common clear-cut ideals for their future, and withal acutely conscious of their distinctness from all other peoples. We may add that they showed what seems to be an almost inseparable mark of nationhood in our own day, the passion to be free, which included for them, as it seems usually to include—as it certainly has included for most of the nations liberated since 1914—freedom to dominate others.

The peoples of the Graeco-Roman world in general may or may not have been acutely conscious of their nationhood—I believe for the most part they were not —but they were certainly conscious that the Jews were a people apart, characterized, as it seemed to them, by *hostile odium adversus omnes*, and they reciprocated this hatred with an anti-semitism which smouldered for long periods and broke out in violence from time to time. In the relations of Jew and Gentile, if not elsewhere in the environment of early Christianity, we have something very like the international enmities which have devastated our world. And if it be said—as I think it must be said with increasing truth—that 'ideological' factors enter largely into such enmities, this is equally true of the enmity of Jew and Gentile. For the Jew, the Greek was an idolater; for the Greek or Roman, the Jew was an atheist. Enough said: *écraser l'infâme!* The enmity broke out into overt war, in the Jewish rebellion of A.D. 66. It was one of the most atrocious wars recorded in ancient history, even though its atrocities may not have been on a scale commensurate with our more advanced civilization. It ended in A.D. 70 with the total defeat of the Jews, the destruction of their capital city, and the end of a Jewish state in Palestine for nineteen centuries. Such was the background against which we must contemplate the early years of Christianity, which began among the Jews and early sought to win the peoples of the Graeco-Roman world.

It may have been actually during the war—in any case it was very near to it in time—that a remarkable pamphlet upon the subject of reconciliation was issued from Christian sources: the pamphlet which we call the Epistle to the Ephesians. It is obviously not so much a letter as a tract or pamphlet cast in the epistolary mould much favoured at that time by writers on philosophical topics. Its dominant theme is the unity designed by God for mankind, and its realization in and through the catholic Church. It ends with one of the most militant passages in the New Testament—that familiar passage which describes the Christian warrior armed with the panoply of God. The soldier of Christ, we are told, is engaged in desperate conflict with 'principalities and powers, the dark tyrants of the universe, and the spiritual forces of wickedness in the unseen world'.[1] We should certainly be wrong in 'etherializing' these enemies overmuch, as if the author were thinking of the lonely struggle of the individual soul against temptations to sin and unbelief. For the Christian of the first century the 'principalities and powers' were very real and concrete. They were embodied in movements and institutions —religious, social and political—which continually threatened the nascent Christian movement with the peril of overwhelming might or seductive propaganda. The fight was real enough and grim enough—as real and grim as the fight against Nazi paganism was for Christians in Germany not many years ago. If we bear this in mind, the picture of the Christian warrior gets

[1] Eph. 6.12.

[22]

firmer outlines. He is to fight the pagan peril armed with truth, justice, faith, and the word of God, and—perhaps surprisingly—'shod with the preparation of the gospel of peace';[1] as if the proclamation of the peace of God were the most effective weapon possible in the war against paganism even in its most material forms. It is worth while recalling that the Church did in fact fight the pagan menace for two hundred and fifty years with precisely these weapons. This superbly militant passage is sufficient to show that the attitude of our author to a world in which injustice and tyranny are abroad is anything but passive or acquiescent, and that his interest in peace and reconciliation does not exclude a resolute defiance of all that is evil in human society.

It is in this work, almost alone in the New Testament, that we have set before us the theme of the reconciliation of two hostile sections of the human race, which we may, if we will, not unfairly describe as two nations. The two parties to be reconciled are the Jews and the Gentiles—whom in this context we may equate with Graeco-Roman society as it was in the first century. The hostility between them, we recall, was no mere *odium theologicum*, such as might perhaps have been cured by a little tolerance and common sense. It was the kind of enmity that culmin-

1 Eph. 6.15.

ated in the horrors of the siege of Jerusalem, perhaps almost as the writer laid down his pen.

With all this in mind, let me read the relevant passage from this remarkable pamphlet. It is addressed to Christian readers drawn from Graeco-Roman circles.

> 'Remember, you Gentiles, that you were at one time aliens from the commonwealth of Israel, and strangers to the charter of its privileges. But now you, once so remote, have been made near neighbours through Christ's self-sacrifice. For He is our peace: He broke through the barrier of enmity that kept us apart, and abolished the rules and restrictions of the ancient law; to create, by making peace, one new humanity out of the two parties, and to reconcile them both to God in one body, through His sufferings on the cross, by which He killed the enmity between us'.[1]

I take this to mean two things, bound up together. On the one hand it treats the creation of the Church, theologically, as a kind of symbolic expression, within history, of an act of God, eternal in quality, crucial and decisive for the whole destiny of man, and as such absolutely unique and unrepeatable. On the other hand it recognizes the remarkable historical fact that there

[1] Eph. 2. 11–15.

[24]

had recently been established, within the Graeco-Roman world, an *enclave* of peace, within which representatives of two 'nations' which at that moment were at one another's throats lived in amity as members of one community; and elucidates the nature of that fact.

With the former, the theological, aspect of the matter I am not here concerned, except to observe that in the Christian view the ultimate hope of the unification of mankind rests upon the reality of the act of God in Christ. But in its historical aspect it refers to a particular event of considerable importance —the effectual overcoming of a long-standing and deep rooted enmity, which we may fairly treat as a model of the process of reconciliation between nations as Christianity understands it. In the reconciliation of Jew and Gentile in the Church three elements are emphasized by Christian writers, all of which I believe are directly applicable to the problem as we have it before us to-day.

1. The two parties were brought to accept a position of parity, and surrendered claims to moral superiority and exclusive privilege. For the Jew, entrance into the Christian community meant the surrender of the ancient institutions of the law of Moses, which he had been taught to consider a mark of God's special favour to his race. That is why our author says so

emphatically that in making peace Christ 'abolished the rules and restrictions of the ancient law'.[1] It was asking a lot of a Jew, to accept that, but it was the condition of any reconciliation. Paul elsewhere expressed it in the maxim, 'There is no distinction', which he enunciates twice in different contexts: 'There is no distinction: all have sinned', and 'There is no distinction: all have the same Lord'.[2] Putting this into terms applicable to a secular situation, we must say, first, that self-righteousness is the bane of international relations. It is this that gives plausibility to the complaint which is sometimes made that attempts to secure reasonable agreements are frustrated by importing irrelevant moral considerations into what should be purely practical matters. If 'moral considerations' means, as it often does, that one nation imposes moral censures or sanctions on another, secure in the persuasion of its own impeccable righteousness, then the complaint is justified. But it would be nearer the truth to say that the first beginning towards reconciliation may often be the acknowledgement by both parties of their responsibility for the evil in the situation: 'all have sinned'. Moreover, 'all have the same Lord'; which means that all nations, whether they recognize it or not, are responsible to the eternal moral law; and this responsibility is bound up with the assurance that the

[1] Eph. 2.15.　　　　[2] Rom. 3.22-23, 10.12

[26]

moral resources and potentialities which the Creator has implanted in our nature are equally available for all peoples. It is on this assumption, and not on the contrary assumption that some peoples are 'good' and others are 'bad' and will always have to be kept in their place by force or guile, that we may hope for true reconciliation.

2. The reconciliation in view was not a matter of politic accommodation between the interests of the two parties, leaving each of them very much where it was before, in the enjoyment of all its independence, power and sovereignty, while cautiously admitting those of the other party. It took the form of the creation of a 'one new humanity'. 'New humanity' is too big a word for any situation with which we are likely to be concerned; but we may fairly say that any effective reconciliation between nations will involve a real new community into which the rivals enter as constituent members, both admitting at least some measure of change in their status. It is at least arguable that our present deadlock is due to the refusal to make the United Nations a *real* community, and to accept the differences that would make to the status of us all.

3. The change which is required is primarily a change of mind (*metanoia*), and not merely a change of conditions or of machinery. In the circumstances in which the Christian reconciliation of Jew and

Gentile took place, the devising of organization or machinery took a subordinate place. It was largely a reconstruction of ideas. And this reconstruction was so effectively carried out, under the stimulus of the Christian gospel, that within the new society Jew and Greek alike could preserve perfect loyalty to, and perfect continuity with, the traditions of his own people, while both entered together into new worlds of thought. It was neither by the conversion of Gentiles into good Jews (as Paul's opponents would have wished), nor by the adoption into a Greek system of a few Jewish ideas (as Gnostics within and without the Church would have had it) that the great intellectual advance represented by early Christian thought was effected. Both those ways proved sterile. The Christian synthesis of Jewish and Gentile thought endured, as the framework within which the mind of man set out on unprecedented explorations. I suggest that in our situation, while politicians and technicians do their necessary work, the most urgent task, if there is to be effective reconciliation in the future, is that of re-thinking our inherited ideas upon such questions as the true ends of human society, the nature and relations of freedom, justice and law, and the true content of human welfare. And here it is the Christian claim that in the Gospel, deeply considered, there reside conceptions still to be explored, suitable

[28]

for shaping a new community of mankind, and that in the ecumenical fellowship of the Church it should be possible to explore them in relative freedom from the distorting influence of narrowly national traditions.

I submit that in these three principles at least we have something which can be directly applied in constructive criticism to all plans for dealing with our urgent problem of reconciliation between nations.

BURGE MEMORIAL LECTURES

still available

S C M PRESS LTD
56 Bloomsbury Street, London, WC1